YOUR WINNING LOTTERY TICKET

Garrett Greiner

1st WORLD
PUBLISHING

Your Winning Lottery Ticket

Garrett Greiner

Copyright © 2022

Published by 1st World Publishing
P.O. Box 2211, Fairfield, Iowa 52556
tel: 641-209-5000 • fax: 866-440-5234
web: www.1stworldpublishing.com

First Edition
ISBN Softcover: 978-1-4218-3525-9
LCCN: Library of Congress Cataloging-in-Publication Data

This material has been written and published for educational purposes to enhance one's well-being. In regard to health issues, the information is not intended as a substitute for appropriate care and advice from health professionals, nor does it equate to the assumption of medical or any other form of liability on the part of the publisher or author. The publisher and author shall have neither liability nor responsibility to any person or entity with respect to loss, damages, or injury claimed to be caused directly or indirectly by any information in this book.

CONTENTS

Mission Statement

The purpose of any mission statement is to communicate the organization/entity's purpose and reason for being. Below I have included several mission statements of the most popular companies in the world and then my own personal mission statement for this book.

> Nike: "To bring inspiration and innovation to every athlete in the world"
>
> Tesla: "To accelerate the world's transition to sustainable energy"
>
> Starbucks: "To inspire and nurture the human spirit – one person, one cup and one neighborhood at a time"
>
> Your Winning Lottery Ticket: "To help any person that picks up a copy of this book improve their life by 1% and discover a slightly better version of themselves and of their life"

If I am able to help make your life 1% better, I believe that 1% will trickle into all aspects of your life which will then trickle down into your community, which will then trickle out into the world. Though it is not the intended effect, it is inevitable that this trickling will eventually come back to me and in turn will make my own life 1% better!

I'm not great at math, but if 1 million people purchase this book and their lives improve just 1% because of it, how does that alter the world? I don't know the answer to that question, but I'd like to find out.

WHAT IS 'YOUR WINNING LOTTERY TICKET'?

This book is intended to serve anyone who wants to live their best life. I believe people purchase lottery tickets because what they truly desire is not some number in a bank account, but rather an improved life, and the freedom to live their best life. In this book you will be given tools to assist you in reaching the next level of your life, and one person who purchases this book and follows the steps outlined in the next chapter will win up to one million dollars.

DECISIONS SHAPE REALITY:

At any moment you can make a decision that could alter your destiny.

"The only thing that changes your life is making decisions."

— Tony Robbins

Exercise: Do not close this book until you have committed to becoming the best version of yourself you can possibly be.

If you are serious about living out the best version of yourself and your life, I ask that you put your money where your mouth is. Throughout this book, you will be asked to fill out the presented journal prompts. These prompts are designed to propel you towards your best self and therefore your best life. What we write down we are more likely to follow through on. If you are committed to making your life 1% better, rewrite the following bolded words in the space below. Rewriting these words is you making a powerful decision, and decisions shape our destiny.

From this day forward, I will not hold any other human more accountable than I will hold myself.

_____

_____

_____

If you have truly accepted this call to greatness, the next time you hear someone complaining about how "XYZ President is ruining this country,' you have to pause and say to them, 'No, I'm ruining it by refusing to step up.'

"If you could kick the person in the pants responsible for most of your trouble, you wouldn't sit for a month."

— Theodore Roosevelt

"You are one decision away from changing your life."

— Anonymous

"Wherever you are, good or bad, is because of the choices you make."

— Lou Holtz

"You will become extraordinary when you make an extraordinary decision."

— Steve Harvey

Exercise: Since I am writing this book to help make your life 1% better, I might as well start by asking you to write on the questions of 'What would make my life 1% better? What could I do today to slightly improve my life?

If I were to spend ten minutes making my life better, what would I have to do?'

_____

_____

_____

_____

_____

_____

_____

Exercise: What decision could you make that could drastically improve your life? What decision could you make right now that could take your life to another level? What is an extraordinary decision that you can make to change your life?

_____
_____
_____
_____
_____
_____
_____
_____
_____
_____

Exercise: What would need to happen for this book to change your life/take your life to the next level? What actions would it need to provoke in you? What decision would you need to make to take your life to the next level?

_____
_____
_____
_____
_____
_____
_____
_____
_____
_____

"Try to make one room in your home as beautiful as possible."

—Jordan Peterson

Exercise: Decide to make one room in your home beautiful. If you can make a room in your house 1% better, you certainly can make your life 1% better. What would make this room more beautiful?

_____

_____

_____

_____

_____

_____

_____

_____

_____

_____

Exercise: The World's Greatest Gift

People often give gifts and other presents to people they care about. I believe the best gift we can give the people we care about is who we become. Think about the people or things you care most about. How could you be better for the people you are about?

_____

_____

_____

_____

_____

_____

_____

_____

_____

_____

Exercise: Write down anything you don't like in your life. Once you have this list, make the decision to not tolerate anything on this list.

_____

_____

_____

_____

_____

_____

_____

_____

_____

_____

_____

_____

_____

_____

_____

_____

_____

_____

_____

_____

_____

_____

_____

_____

_____

_____

_____

_____

_____

Exercise: Every decision you make will help or hurt your confidence. Write down decisions you are making that hurt your confidence. What decisions make you more confident?

_____

_____

_____

_____

_____

_____

_____

_____

_____

THE LAW OF ATTRACTION

What is the law of attraction and how can you use it to get what you want? The law of attraction is the notion that with the power of your mind and the power of your thoughts you have the ability to shape your world. It's the understanding that your mind can and does shift reality, and if you learn to control your mind you can create virtually whatever you desire. The law of attraction is the belief that you are able to create whatever situation that you want for yourself.

Using the power of your mind to create things is not about disregarding your present reality. Rather, it's understanding that your mind and your thoughts have the power to shape reality.

The law of attraction gets a bad reputation because in trying to get people to understand that their thoughts have physical power, there was a miscommunication that thoughts are all that is required. In James 2:14-26, it is written, "Faith by itself, if it is not accompanied by action, is dead." You can create whatever it is you want, but no matter what you want, it will not come without action. **If you want something, you can have it, if you act in alignment with what you want.**

Where focus goes, energy flows. Where energy flows, reality grows.

Your repetitive thoughts hold creation power

"Whatever is going on in your mind you're attracting to you, by the images you hold in your mind. Thoughts become things. If you see it in your head, you can hold it in your hand."

— Bob Proctor

"I saw it so clearly, I swear to god I saw it so clearly, so consistently, and so frequently it has manifested itself into reality."

— Conor McGregor

"You are a magnet attracting what you think and feel."

— Anonymous

"Whatever you hold in your mind on a consistent basis is exactly what you will experience in your life."

— Tony Robbins

"If you can think about what you want in your mind, and make that your dominant thought, you will draw it into your life."

— Rhonda Byrne

"The key to success and the key to failure is, we become what we think about."

— Earl Nightingale

"Every single thought manifests."

— Lester Levenson

"A man is literally what he thinks, his character being the com-

plete sum of all his thoughts. You are today where your thoughts have brought you; you will be tomorrow where your thoughts take you."

— James Allen

"*The words we speak, the things we say, it's like you're building your road with those words.*"

— Alicia Keys

"*As a man thinketh in his heart, so shall he be.*"

— Proverbs 23:7

"Watch your thoughts—they become your words; watch your words—they become your actions; watch your actions—they become your habits; watch your habits—they become your character; watch your character—it becomes your destiny."

— Lao Tzu

"*I found that when you start thinking and saying what you really want, then your mind automatically shifts and pulls you in that direction. And sometimes it can be that simple; just a little twist in vocabulary that illustrates your attitude and philosophy.*"

— Jim Rohn

"*A man's life is what his thoughts make of it.*"

— Marcus Aerelius

"*A man is what he thinks about all day long.*"

— Ralph Waldo Emerson

"A man is but the product of his thoughts. What he thinks, he becomes."

— Mahatma Gandhi

"You have heard that it was said, 'You shall not commit adultery.' But, I tell you that any man that imagines a woman lustfully has already committed adultery with her in his heart."

— Matthew 5: 27-28:

"As a single footstep will not make a path on the earth, so a single thought will not make a pathway in the mind. To make a deep physical path, we walk again and again. To make a deep mental path, we must think over and over the kind of thoughts we wish to dominate our lives."

— Wilfred Arlan Peterson

Exercise: This journal prompt will help you shift your thoughts into alignment with your desire. Picture in your mind your ideal life. Spend a few minutes writing about what it would mean to think in alignment with that. What are your current dominating thoughts? If you were living in alignment with the person you wanted to be and the life you wanted to live, what would your dominant thoughts be? What would somebody who has that life consistently be thinking? What would they not be thinking? What new thoughts would you need to start thinking that would bring you in alignment with what you want? How can you better align your dominant thoughts and attitudes with your desire? Write down the thoughts you cannot bring to your future.

_____
_____
_____
_____

_____
_____
_____
_____
_____
_____
_____
_____
_____
_____
_____
_____
_____
_____
_____
_____
_____
_____
_____
_____
_____
_____
_____
_____
_____
_____
_____
_____
_____
_____
_____
_____

Ask, Believe, Receive:

"Whatever things you ask for in prayer, believe that you have received them, and you shall have them."

— Jesus

"Faith is to believe what you do not see; the reward of this faith is to see what you believe."

— Saint Augustine

"You must feel the feelings of your wish fulfilled and continue feeling that it is fulfilled until that which you feel objectifies itself. Call your desires into being by imagining and feeling your wish fulfilled"

— Neville Goddard

"Visualize your goal, something you want to achieve and really get into the state of having already acquired it."

— John Asaraf

"I believe in putting a rocket ship of desire into the universe and you get it when you believe it, you get it when you believe you have it."

— Jim Carrey

"Teach your body emotionally what that future feels like before it happens. Define yourself by a vision of the future, rather than the memories of the past. If you change how you think, act, or feel, you change your life. When you get into the state of having it already, your brain and body are physically changed as though the experience has already occurred. Your brain then becomes a road

map to the future, rather than a record of the past. "

— Dr. Joe Dispenza

"I don't want to be anything, I am everything I want to be, I am already there. If the vibe you're putting out is want, you're always going to want, I always have the attitude I have. I don't want anything, I have everything… You can almost visually create your entire world, not almost, you actually can. Then I was like, I'm going to do that, and I will do that, and that's when I began to practice it."

—Conor Mcgregor

"Each day, close your eyes for several minutes and visualize already having what you want, and feeling the feelings of already having it."

— Jack Canfield

"Assume that you are already what you want to be, then live by faith in this assumption. Make your future dream a present fact by assuming the feeling of your wish fulfilled."

— Wayne Dyer

"The just shall live by faith."

— Romans 1:17

"Every feeling makes a subconscious impression."

— Dr. Joseph Murphy

In '*Believe In Yourself*' by Dr. Joseph Murphy, he writes that 'Joseph' in the Bible means 'well-disciplined imagination'. A well-disciplined imagination is the ability to hold your desire in your imagination until its fulfillment, regardless of your present reality. It takes faith to hold onto the feeling of your wish already having been fulfilled, especially when your current physical reality does not match up with that.

"*At the end of the day you have to feel some type of way. Why not feel like the person you want to be?*"

— Anonymous

Anytime you ever desire anything, regardless of how big or small it is—whether it's a parking space, making a certain amount of money, or putting a human on Mars—your job is to believe it's yours, and get into the state of already having it now. Your ability to remain in the state of your wish having been fulfilled and continue acting in alignment with what you want over the long term requires deep faith and will lead you to creating what you want. The stronger and more consistently you feel the feeling of that wish fulfilled, the greater your chances in getting to that reality.

Complex formula that only the elite put into practice:

Step 1: Desire it. Ask for what you want. Ask with maximum clarity.

Step 2: Get into the state of already having received your desire.

Step 3: Take inspired action. You don't need to see the whole picture, just take the steps you know you need to take.

Step 4: Receive it.

Remember, "Blessed are those who have not seen and yet have believed." John 20:29

Exercise: Close your eyes and get into the state of already having, being, and doing, everything you ever wanted. Get into that state of your wish being fulfilled. Get into the state of your prayer already answered and remain in that state for several minutes. After several minutes, open your eyes, and follow your intuition.

"You miss 100% of the attempts you never take."

— Wayne Gretzky

Exercise: Whatever you want most in life, make 10 attempts. Make 100 attempts. Keep making attempts until you can't make any more!

Step 1: Write down something you deeply desire:

_____

_____

_____

_____

Step 2: Make a hundred attempts

Step 3: If that wasn't enough, make a thousand attempts and see what happens.

	Failures	Successes
Many Attempts	𝍸𝍸𝍸𝍸𝍸𝍸𝍸 𝍸𝍸𝍸𝍸𝍸𝍸𝍸	𝍸
No attempts	None	N/A

Affirmations: The Power of Words

"Whosoever shall say to his mountain be removed, be cast into the sea, and shall not doubt in his heart but shall believe those things that he said shall come to pass—he shall have whatsoever he said."

— Mark 11:23

"The power of life and death is in the tongue."

— Proverbs 18:21

"I feel that things that I repeatedly think about or say, I'm able to manifest."

— Drake

"I've done affirmations for a long time. I believe that your thoughts create your life."

— Jennifer Lopez

"The words that follow 'I am' follow you."

— Anonymous

"You are whatever you tell yourself that you are."

— Conor Mcgregor

"I am the greatest. I told myself that even before I knew I was."

— Muhammad Ali

Romans 4:17 *"God calleth those things which be not as though they were."*

Exercise: If you want to be more like God, begin by calling the things that are not as though they were. Turn your goals into affirmations and say them in the present tense. Speak these desires knowing that your tongue has the power of life and death. When you speak it, feel the feelings of that affirmation being true.

Write down your ten most important goals:
Example goal: Make one million dollars

_____

_____

_____

_____

_____

_____

_____

_____

_____

_____

Next, transform these goals into affirmations so that you can call the things that are not, as though they were, and in that sense you begin acting out who you truly are, a child of God.

Goals Transformed into affirmations to say at least once daily:

Example affirmation: I am a millionaire. I provide so much value to others that I easily make millions of dollars.

_____

_____

_____

_____

_____

_____

_____

_____

_____

Exercise: This journal prompt will help you align your beliefs with your desired reality and shift your thoughts into alignment with your desire. Picture in your mind your ideal life. Spend a few minutes writing about what it would mean to think in alignment with that. What would your dominant thoughts need to be? How can you alter your dominant thoughts/beliefs to better align yourself with this life?

_____

_____

_____

_____

_____

_____

_____

_____

Exercise: This journal prompt will help you shift your actions into alignment with your desire. Picture in your mind your ideal life. Spend a few minutes writing about what it would mean to act in alignment with that? What would somebody who has that life consistently be doing? What would they not be doing? How can you better align yourself with this life?

_____

_____

_____

_____

_____

_____

_____

_____

_____

_____

The Power Of Identity:

"I see myself as the champ already. I've seen myself as the champ from day one. Before I even started training, I saw myself as the champ. All that matters is how you see yourself. If you see yourself as the King, with all the belts, and all everything, if you see that, and really believe in it, then no matter what anyone else says, that's what's going to happen. Who can tell you otherwise? Who can tell you what you see through your own eyes? Nobody, that's who. Nobody but you! I said this long before my UFC debut fight in an old MTV documentary I did. Early, early days. How wild! Be who you know you are."

— Conor Mcgregor

Why not identify yourself with the person you want to be? Transgender people do it, and will get offended if you don't accept their reality. Regardless of your viewpoints, this can teach us a valuable lesson: Identify as the person you truly want to be, begin acting in alignment with it, and make others accept your reality. With your combination of identity and actions, you will begin bringing it into your reality.

Whoever you want to be, start identifying yourself as that person right now and then begin acting in alignment with that. Begin holding yourself to the standards that this version of yourself would be held to.

Exercise: The following writing prompts are designed to help you gain clarity on who you want to be. "Make a written description of the person you're about to become. Write down with as much detail as possible who you want to be. If you could make a wish and become the version of yourself that you dreamed of being, what would that look like? Spend the next several minutes writing about who you want to be, and write it in the present tense." — Bob Proctor

I am so filled with joy and passion that I am:

_____
_____
_____
_____
_____
_____
_____
_____
_____
_____
_____
_____
_____
_____
_____
_____
_____
_____
_____
_____
_____
_____
_____

Exercise part 2: Imagine the person you deeply want to become and hold that image in your mind. Now, fill out the following prompt as though you are already the person you desire to be.

I'm the type of person that (Write down whatever the person you want to be would say).

I'm the type of person that _____

_____

I'm the type of person that_____

_____

I'm the type of person that_____

_____

I'm the type of person that_____

_____

I'm the type of person that_____

_____

I'm the type of person that_____

_____

I'm the type of person that_____

_____

I'm the type of person that_____

_____

I'm the type of person that_____

_____

I'm the type of person that_____

_____

I'm the type of person that_____

_____

I'm the type of person that_____

_____

I'm the type of person that_____

_____

I'm the type of person that_____

_____

I'm the type of person that_____

_____

I'm the type of person that_____

_____

I'm the type of person that_____

_____

I'm the type of person that_____

_____

I'm the type of person that_____

_____

I'm the type of person that_____

_____

I'm the type of person that_____

_____

I'm the type of person that_____

_____

The Power Of Identity:

I'm the type of person that_____

_____

I'm the type of person that_____

_____

I'm the type of person that_____

_____

I'm the type of person that_____

_____

I'm the type of person that_____

_____

I'm the type of person that_____

_____

I'm the type of person that_____

_____

I'm the type of person that_____

_____

I'm the type of person that_____

_____

I'm the type of person that_____

_____

I'm the type of person that_____

_____

I'm the type of person that_____

_____

I'm the type of person that_____
_____

I'm the type of person that_____
_____

I'm the type of person that_____
_____

"*Whatever people have their identity attached to, they live. We live who we believe we are. Once you decide who you are, that behavior will become consistent. The strongest force in the human personality is this need to stay consistent with how we define ourselves. Change your identity and your behavior will follow.*"

— Tony Robbins

"*We live by what we believe.*"

—2 Corinthians 5:7-17

Exercise: Imagine who you could be, and begin to act as though you are already that person. How would the person you want to become act? Act that way. If your goal is to be fit, what would a fit person do? If your goal is to be rich, what would a rich person do?

_____
_____
_____
_____
_____
_____
_____
_____
_____
_____

Now that you know how the person you want to be would act, begin to act that way. You have to act some way; why not act like the person you want to be?

Aligning actions with desired reality: What action(s) would I need to consistently implement to be in alignment with what I want?

_____

_____

_____

_____

_____

_____

_____

_____

_____

CONSTANTLY LEARNING

"Formal education will make you a living; self-education will make you a fortune."

— Jim Rohn

"What drives me today is being my best, and being my best is a neverending journey."

— David Goggins

"Live as if you were to die tomorrow. Learn as if you were to live forever."

— Mahatma Gandhi

"I've never met someone so stupid I couldn't learn from them."

— Galileo Galilei

"Anyone who stops learning is old—whether this happens at twenty or eighty. Anyone who keeps on learning not only remains young but becomes constantly more valuable."

— Henry Ford

In the previous section, we talked about identity. If you want to identify yourself with being a massive winner, you must accept continuous learning as a part of your destiny.

Winners/champions/leaders/innovators/great people take something from everything, and learn from everything. Regardless of the
quality of this book, if you are truly a winner, you will take away
something that you can apply in your own life. If you identify as a
winner, it's impossible for you to not find at least some value in this
book, because winners take something from everything.

Exercise: Continuous Learning: Imagine the best version of yourself.
What would the best version of yourself like to learn more about in
the next six months? Two years? Five years?

_____

_____

_____

_____

_____

_____

_____

_____

_____

_____

_____

_____

BE A GREAT COPIER

Chamath Palihapitiya: "A lot of my life is just copying things that I see. There's not a lot of original thought here. We can all pretend we're all f***ing geniuses. Honestly, be good copiers. It's the best thing in the world. Be around high functioning, high quality people, and copy the sh** that they do. Observe the sh** that's crappy, and don't do that stuff. It's not a f***ing complicated formula."

Exercise: Decide for yourself. Think about the people you respect the most, and those that you don't respect at all. What do they do that makes you feel this way? What do you like/dislike about them? What are you going to embody? What are you going to copy? What are you not going to copy?

_____

_____

_____

_____

_____

_____

Translation: Monkey see monkey do. If you see a monkey with a lot of chocolate bars, and you want a lot of chocolate bars, do what the monkey with a lot of chocolate bars is doing, but slightly better!

There is some area of your life you want to be successful in, whether it's conscious or unconscious. Imagine someone who is already successful in that area. What is something you can emulate from them? What are several consistent actions this person is taking?

_____

_____

_____

_____

_____

_____

"A good artist copies; a great artist steals."

— Pablo Picasso

This is one of my favorite quotes because it's a reminder that groundbreaking, world-changing, revolutionary ideas are often the result of taking something that already exists, and making it slightly better, changing some small thing about it in order to serve someone else.

The story of Tinder and Bumble. The founder of Bumble is the world's youngest female self made-billionaire. Did she have some revolutionary idea? No. She was dating the founder of Tinder. She had the blueprint, she had the model, she had the recipe for the cake. Her ex evidently pissed her off enough that she said with her actions, 'F*** you. I have the recipe, I'm going to copy the recipe, but I'm going to make my cake yellow, and I'm going to market it towards women.' After some time of playing around with any recipe you get more comfortable with it and continue adding additional tweaks. Eventually she added chocolate chips, and another egg to make it more fluffy. That to me is a perfect example of this quote. From my perspective, she clearly got the basis of her recipe from Tinder, but she added her own touch and in doing so made it her own. She did such a good job with her cake that the majority of people will never know, or will never care where the basis of the recipe came from. Her bank account certainly doesn't care. In my eyes and I believe in Pablo Picasso's, she became his definition of a great artist.

Other great rivalries: Nike, Reebok, Adidas, New Balance, Underarmour. Disney, Hulu, Netflix. Bank of America, Wells Fargo,

Chase, Capital One. Southwest, American Airlines, United, Spirit. Uber Eats, Doordash, Grubhub. Tesla, GM, Ford. The list goes on and on. The point being, none of these companies are revolutionary when looking at the other companies in their industry. Tesla didn't invent the electric car, they simply created a better version of it. Being successful in business and in life is about making incremental positive alterations to something that already exists and or something you're already doing. You don't have to come up with the next big idea, you just have to improve upon what already exists.

Exercise: What is something that you are currently doing in your life, that you can make incremental positive alterations to? What is something you can make slight improvements to, or present in a new way to better serve yourself or those around you?

_____

_____

_____

_____

_____

_____

Note: Copyright infringement and other laws exist to keep people from straight up copying, and not adding any extra value on top of it. I'm not advocating for copying, I am advocating for constant incremental improvements.

"We're not competitor obsessed, we're customer obsessed."

— Jeff Bezos

If any of the companies listed above want to remain the top dog, they MUST place a continual focus on quality, affordability, and serving their customers the absolute best they can. Business is about competing to serve customers. The company that wins the game, the company that gets to continue to exist, is the company that serves their customers the best.

Exercise: Business and Wealth creation are about making constant improvements over time in order to deliver more value. In your own line of work, your hobbies, or whatever arena you spend much of your time in, how can you create an incremental improvement in something you currently do? How can you make something you are currently involved in just 1% better? 1% more valuable? How can you do what you currently do 1% better?

_____

_____

_____

_____

_____

_____

_____

_____

_____

_____

_____

_____

_____

_____

_____

_____

BE GREAT WHEREVER YOU ARE

I believe this statement is the key to success in life, and if I could only leave one principle behind it would be this.

If you are only going to remember one thing from this book, let it be this simple statement. 'Be Great Wherever You are.' This is the 'secret sauce' that the richest people in history share.

Everybody we admire is great at something.

"If a man is called a street sweeper, he should sweep streets as Michelangelo painted, or Beethoven composed music, or Shakespeare wrote poetry. He should sweep streets so well that all the hosts of heaven and Earth will pause to say, here lived a great street sweeper who did his job well."

— Martin Luther King Jr.

Whatever you do, wherever you are, be great at it, and eventually good things will happen. Find something you enjoy doing, something that fulfills you, gives you meaning, and become great at it. The process of mastery can be fulfilling and addictive.

Exercise: What do you enjoy doing? What fulfills you? What gives you a sense of meaning and purpose? What lights you up? What puts a smile on your face? What do you want to be the best in the world at? What do you want to be great at? What is most beneficial for you to become great at? Why?

_____

_____

_____

_____

_____

_____

_____

_____

_____

_____

_____

_____

_____

_____

Pursue excellence in all that you do, and eventually your bank account will look excellent too.

"Your country is starving for you to step up and become fucking great."

— Andy Frisella

Tools to be great wherever you are:

If you're reading this book, it means you are probably a winner. Since you're a winner, the result we're after is greatness wherever you are.

Exercise: There is no shortage of reasons to be great. Write for several minutes on the question of, 'What are some reasons for me to be great? If I were all I could be, how might I benefit? How might others I care about benefit? How might the world benefit?

_____

———————————————————————————
———————————————————————————
———————————————————————————
———————————————————————————
———————————————————————————
———————————————————————————
———————————————————————————
———————————————————————————

Exercise: In this section, I ask that you commit to being great wherever you are. If you're not willing to make that commitment, you might as well close the book right now. (The haters that say this book isn't helpful aren't willing to make the commitment. If you are someone who makes the commitment and still thinks this book isn't great, think again. I got you to commit to greatness.

Write down below '**I commit to being great wherever I am, no matter what life throws at me.**' Then continue on.

———————————————————————————
———————————————————————————
———————————————————————————

"Whatever you do, do it better than anybody that ever did it before. If your job is to get the coffee, make it better than anybody ever did it before. Everything works itself out if you function that way."

—Josh Mcdaniels

"Whatever job you do, do it like you own the company."

— Richard Montañez

"If you endeavor to clean your room, clean your room like you're a teenage boy, and the hottest girl in school is coming over to study."

— Anonymous

"Do your job, do your mission like your childhood hero is watching you all day long."

— Anonymous

Whatever you do, do it like the people you most admire, do it like God himself is watching you. Imagine God is watching you all day, every day. Some people don't like the word God. If that's you, picture meeting the ten people you admire or respect the most, and imagine that feeling multiplied by a million. In fact, if you truly ever met God you would probably have a heart attack from the nervousness. Imagine the person you want to make so proud is watching you in everything you do.

Exercise: Successful people, whether working for themselves or somebody else, alone, or in a crowd, do whatever they do to the best of their ability. Excellence is a choice. Whatever career field you are in, what would it look like if you were committed to being excellent? What would it look like if you were the best in the world at it? How would you benefit? How would others benefit?

_____

_____

_____

_____

_____

_____

"Stop complaining, differentiate yourself from the competition. Ducks quack and complain. Eagles soar above the crowd."

— Wayne Dyer

Exercise: If you were going to stop quacking like a duck and start soaring like an eagle, what would that look like? What would you have to do to be more like an eagle than a duck? What could you do today to lean into being an eagle and lean away from being a duck?

_____
_____
_____
_____
_____
_____
_____

"You cannot be jealous of someone or something you don't truly desire. Jealousy is a clue, it's a directional signal. Instead of aiming jealousy at the world, turn it into inspiration. Your jealousy isn't going away—it will either consume you, or you will empower yourself to start moving towards what you want. The people and things you are jealous of are your guide posts."

— Mel Robbins

Exercise: What makes you jealous? What is it exactly about that thing that makes you jealous?

_____
_____
_____
_____
_____
_____
_____

What is this jealousy trying to tell you?

_____
_____
_____
_____
_____
_____
_____

Aim at Something

"Where there is no vision, the people perish."

— Proverbs 29:18

"The most important thing is that you have a vision, that you have a goal, because without that vision and without that goal, you're drifting around and you're never going to end up anywhere. Discover your vision and the rest will follow."

— Arnold Schwarzenegger

"We all have a choice: we can either make a living, or design a life. The major reason for setting a goal is what it makes of you. What it makes of you will always be of far greater value than what you get."

— Jim Rohn

"If you don't know what you're doing, aim at something. Is it the right thing? No, but it's better than just shooting randomly. Aim at something that would be an accomplishment, something that would make you proud."

— Jordan Peterson

"The republic is a dream, and if we don't keep dreaming, we will lose the republic."

— Ronald Reagan

"If your dreams don't scare you, they aren't big enough."

— Muhammad Ali

Exercise: What is the highest good you can aim at? If you were aiming at something that was meaningful to you, what would that look like? How can you readjust your current aim to make it a 1% better aim?

_____

_____

_____

_____

_____

_____

"The main thing is to be proud of yourself when you're by yourself."

— Anonymous

The people we care about can be a massive source of inspiration. Picture someone you care deeply about, someone you want to make proud. How could you be just 1% better for them?

_____

_____

_____

_____

_____

_____

_____

"Only surround yourself with people that inspire you."

— Ben Nemtin

Exercise: Imagine it is your birthday five years from now. If you're currently thirty, imagine it is your thirty-fifth birthday. On this future birthday when you are looking back over the previous five years, what would make you proud of yourself? What would make you say, 'These past five years have been so meaningful'?

_____

_____

_____

_____

_____

_____

_____

_____

_____

_____

_____

_____

_____

_____

_____

_____

_____

_____

_____

"The effect you have on others is the most valuable currency there is."

—Jim Carrey

Giving to others can be one of the most rewarding and fulfilling activities we do. How are you currently helping others? How could you do that 1% better? How would you like to help others in the future?

_____

_____

_____

_____

_____

_____

_____

_____

_____

End in mind thinking: What do you want? What would make it addictively compelling? How do you align yourself with what you want as you begin moving towards it? What must be true if you are to end up where you want to go?

_____

_____

_____

_____

_____

_____

_____

_____

Be A Workhorse

"The price of success is hard work, dedication to the job at hand, and the determination that whether we win or lose, we have applied the best of ourselves to the task at hand. The dictionary is the only place that success comes before work. Work is the key to success, and hard work can help you accomplish anything."

— Vince Lombardi

"Talent is cheaper than table salt. What separates the talented individual from the successful one is a lot of hard work."

— Stephen King

"All roads that lead to success have to pass through hard work boulevard at some point."

— Eric Thomas

One of the goals of this chapter is to shift the reader's mindset from 'going to work', to working towards something. You aren't 'going to work', you are working towards something. Clarify what you want, imagine a beautiful vision, a beautiful life that you want to live, and then begin working towards it.

Exercise: What are you working towards? Why? Why do you benefit? Why do others benefit?

_____

_____

_____

_____

_____

_____

"My business philosophy is work harder than everyone else."

—Jennifer Lopez

"Satisfaction lies in the effort, not in the attainment. Full effort is full victory."

— Mahatma Gandhi

"You can outwork anybody, no matter how badass they are, because work ethic is a choice."

—Anonymous

"My work ethic came from my father. I don't know anybody who works harder than I do. I'm working all the time. It's not about the money—I just don't know a different way of life, and I love it."

—Donald Trump

"Your work is going to fill a large part of your life, and the only way to be truly satisfied is to do what you believe is great work, and the only way to do great work is to love what you do."

—Steve Jobs

"Hard work is a prison sentence only if it does not have meaning. Once it does, it becomes the kind of thing that makes you grab your wife around the waist and dance a jig. If you work hard enough and assert yourself, and use your mind and imagination, you can shape the world to your desires."

— Malcolm Gladwell

"I believe in hard work and luck, and that the first often leads to the second."

— J.K. Rowling

"People don't understand that when I grew up, I was never the most talented. I was never the biggest. I was never the fastest. I certainly was never the strongest. The only thing I had was my work ethic, and that's been what has gotten me this far."

—Tiger Woods

"You can flex work ethic, there is no budget, you can't go broke on it, it's never going to be bad for you. Driven is a huge asset if you can tap into it."

— Grant Cardone

"I never took a day off in my twenties. Not one."

— Bill Gates

"Be humble, be hungry, and be the hardest worker in the room."

— Dwayne 'The Rock' Johnson.

"Work as hard at your job as you can for six weeks, flat out, and see what happens. Work as hard as you possibly can on one thing and see what happens. Those that work 10% longer hours make 40% more money."

— Jordan Peterson

"There is no big secret. Whatever your goal for this year is, you can get there—as long as you're willing to be honest with yourself about the preparation and work involved. There are no back doors, no free rides... If you decide to rise up and create a new experience for yourself, I know for sure that you can attain it the old-fashioned way—through hard work."

— Oprah Winfrey

A single draft horse can pull a load up to 8,000 pounds. Two draft horses pulling together cannot pull twice as much as one, they can actually pull three times as much. The two draft horses that can each pull 8,000 pounds alone can pull 24,000 pounds working together. This is used to illustrate that work ethic is not linear. (https://tim-maurer.com/2012/01/16/horse-sense/)

Exercise: Challenge: Many of the most admired people in history had a great work ethic. Challenge: For the next eight weeks, in whatever avenue you choose, pick one thing and work harder than you've ever worked before. Make sure to choose something that will benefit yourself and others—you're not working hard for nothing! Over the next six weeks you will be the workhorse. What will you work on with laser beam intensity?

_____

_____

_____

_____

_____

_____

DELAY GRATIFICATION

People will do almost anything to seek pleasure and avoid pain. People will do almost anything if there is enough of a reward behind it.

> *"I hated every minute of training, but I said, 'Don't quit. Suffer now and live the rest of your life as a champion.'"*
>
> — Muhammad Ali

Delaying gratification is the key to success in life.

Humans have known for thousands of years about the power of delayed gratification. Those with the ability to delay gratification have a lower divorce rate, higher income, better academic results, higher tolerance of stress, better ability to plan and reason, and exhibit greater self control. These studies prove what should be common knowledge: delayed gratification=good.

Exercise: Since we know that delayed gratification is good, journal for a few minutes on the following question before continuing on. "How can you better practice delayed gratification in your own life? How can you better train yourself to delay gratification?

_____

_____

_____

_____

_____

_____

_____

Identify your meaningful rewards: Is it watching TV? Movies? Social events? Food? Once you've identified them, rather than just giving yourself one of these, make yourself earn it. Before you can watch a movie with friends, you have to do XYZ or one of your most important priorities. What are your meaningful rewards?

_____

_____

_____

_____

_____

Exercise: Set up simple intentional rewards for yourself. Write for a few minutes about how you could make your reward system better. What are some specific behaviors you want to reward? How can you set up the reward in such a way where you will want to do those behaviors again, and again, and again? What is your desired behavior and what would it take for you to get to the point where you actually crave doing your desired behavior? How would you need to structure your reward so that you crave doing that behavior again? Are the rewards you currently have for yourself serving your life and your goals? How could you improve the reward process you are giving yourself?

_____

_____

_____

_____

_____

_____

CHALLENGE YOURSELF

"Everyday I do something to scare myself."

— Hellen Keller

"Challenge yourself; it's the only path which leads to growth."

— Morgan Freeman

"You should never view your challenges as a disadvantage. Instead, it's important for you to understand that your experience facing and overcoming adversity is actually one of your biggest advantages."

— Michelle Obama

"It's what you do with your struggle that makes you who you are."

— Anonymous

There is a story about a homeowner who wanted a house cat to keep mice away. The owner brought a kitten into her home and every day would feed it, water it, and change its litter box. After some time, this kitten had grown up, and its belly had grown up too. This now adult kitten was, by all accounts, obese. The frustrated owner wondered why she was still having mice problems so she bought a camera to see what this cat was doing all day. She found that the cat and mouse crossed paths often, but the cat simply didn't seem interested. The moral of the story is that the kitten had been pampered, and was never challenged, and because of that never had to develop. Most people know this truth to be obvious, and yet feel overwhelmed in the face of challenge. The next time you face a challenge, do not feel overwhelmed. Challenges, no matter how impenetrable they may seem, allow us the opportunity to grow stronger than we ever could have been before.

What you stress over, if you do not kill it, you give the opportunity to grow stronger.

Exercise: What are some ways you can integrate stress positively into your life so that you don't end up like the fat cat in the above story?

_____

_____

_____

_____

_____

_____

"Keep challenging yourself to think better, do better, and be better."

— Robin Sharma

"Everything negative—pressure, challenges—is all an opportunity for me to rise."

— Kobe Bryant

"When I say life doesn't happen to you, it happens for you, I really don't know if that's true. I'm just making a conscious choice to perceive challenges as something beneficial so that I can deal with them in the most productive way."

— Jim Carrey

"Do something everyday that sucks."

— David Goggins

Exercise: People become strong by facing challenges, by voluntarily exposing themselves to challenges in incremental doses that they can manage.

The exercise is simple, but not easy. Every day. do something to scare yourself/challenge yourself.

What can you do to challenge yourself? What is the scariest/most challenging thing you can think of doing? What makes you uncomfortable? What will you do today that sucks?

_____

_____

_____

_____

_____

_____

_____

_____

_____

_____

_____

_____

_____

"That which you most need will be found where you least want to look."

— Carl Jung.

Exercise: We know that facing challenges in pieces we can manage makes us stronger. What challenges can you face that would make your life better? Where do you least want to look? What could happen if you faced where you didn't want to and survived? What is the worst case scenario?

_____
_____
_____
_____
_____
_____

Identify a challenge, obstacle, or anything negative in your life. How could this be turned into an opportunity for you?

_____
_____
_____
_____
_____
_____
_____

"It's not what happens to you in life, but how you react to it that matters."

— Epictetus

"No matter your position, circumstances, or opportunities in life, you always have the freedom of mind to choose how you experience, interpret, and ultimately shape your world."

— Brendon Burchard

Picture something painful in your life—something that is not serving you. What is the meaning you are currently giving to that thing? If you were able to give a new meaning to that thing so that it could serve you, what meaning would you need to attach to it?

_____
_____
_____
_____

Budget:

"What gets measured gets improved."

— Peter Drucker

"The rich invest their money and spend what is left; the poor spend their money and invest what is left."

— Jim Rohn

Money is a primary concern for many people, yet most people don't know where their money is going. If you're not currently in control of your finances, improve them by 1% by tracking your money!

January			
Expected Income	Expected Expenses:	Actual Income	Actual Expenses
Salary	Food		
Dividend/invest-ment	Housing		
Royalties	Utilities		
Side Hustle	Transportation		
	Insurance		
	Investments		

February			
Expected Income	Expected Expenses:	Actual Income	Actual Expenses
Salary	Food		
Dividend/invest-ment	Housing		
Royalties	Utilities		
Side Hustle	Transportation		
	Insurance		
	Investments		

March			
Expected Income	Expected Expenses:	Actual Income	Actual Expenses
Salary	Food		
Dividend/invest-ment	Housing		
Royalties	Utilities		
Side Hustle	Transportation		
	Insurance		
	Investments		

April			
Expected Income	Expected Expenses:	Actual Income	Actual Expenses
Salary	Food		
Dividend/invest-ment	Housing		
Royalties	Utilities		
Side Hustle	Transportation		
	Insurance		
	Investments		

May			
Expected Income	Expected Expenses:	Actual Income	Actual Expenses
Salary	Food		
Dividend/invest-ment	Housing		
Royalties	Utilities		
Side Hustle	Transportation		
	Insurance		
	Investments		

June			
Expected Income	Expected Expenses:	Actual Income	Actual Expenses
Salary	Food		
Dividend/investment	Housing		
Royalties	Utilities		
Side Hustle	Transportation		
	Insurance		
	Investments		

July			
Expected Income	Expected Expenses:	Actual Income	Actual Expenses
Salary	Food		
Dividend/investment	Housing		
Royalties	Utilities		
Side Hustle	Transportation		
	Insurance		
	Investments		

August			
Expected Income	Expected Expenses:	Actual Income	Actual Expenses
Salary	Food		
Dividend/investment	Housing		
Royalties	Utilities		
Side Hustle	Transportation		
	Insurance		
	Investments		

September			
Expected Income	Expected Expenses:	Actual Income	Actual Expenses
Salary	Food		
Dividend/invest-ment	Housing		
Royalties	Utilities		
Side Hustle	Transportation		
	Insurance		
	Investments		

October			
Expected Income	Expected Expenses:	Actual Income	Actual Expenses
Salary	Food		
Dividend/invest-ment	Housing		
Royalties	Utilities		
Side Hustle	Transportation		
	Insurance		
	Investments		

November			
Expected Income	Expected Expenses:	Actual Income	Actual Expenses
Salary	Food		
Dividend/invest-ment	Housing		
Royalties	Utilities		
Side Hustle	Transportation		
	Insurance		
	Investments		

December			
Expected Income	Expected Expenses:	Actual Income	Actual Expenses
Salary	Food		
Dividend/investment	Housing		
Royalties	Utilities		
Side Hustle	Transportation		
	Insurance		
	Investments		

Journal Prompts:

What fulfills you? What lights you on fire? What puts a smile on your face? Start vague.

_____

_____

_____

_____

_____

_____

_____

If life were perfect, what would happen next?

_____

_____

_____

_____

_____

_____

_____

_____

_____

_____

"The definition of insanity is doing the same thing over and over again, and expecting a different result."

— Albert Einstein

"If you want to change what you're getting, you have to change what you're doing."

—Brad Lea

Picture an area of your life you're not satisfied with. What if you did the opposite for a week? What can you change that would improve your life?

_____
_____
_____
_____
_____

What would you want to do, have and be if you had ten million dollars? What would your dream life look like if you didn't have to worry about money? If you had the ability to just lie in bed and never had to do anything ever again, what would you want to be doing? (You're just craving to say travel and hobbies aren't you ;))

_____
_____
_____
_____
_____
_____
_____
_____
_____
_____

Exercise: Spend a few minutes writing before continuing on. Imagine the following and describe what you would do: We live in a society where every person is required to work 520 hours a year, or just ten hours a week at something productively and the rest of the time is yours to do with as you please. If you finish your quota in five weeks, the rest of the year is yours to do as you please. Everyone in the community is required to be productive just 520 hours a year and then you have all the freedom you could ever want. In this world, all of your basic needs and then some are provided by the government. Since you are required to work 520 hours a year, what would you want to work on? What would you want to improve upon? How would you like to add value to others? How would you like to be productive?

_____

_____

_____

_____

_____

_____

_____

_____

_____

_____

In your current work, what would be required for you to get more done in less time? How could you be more efficient, and more effective?

_____

_____

_____

_____

_____

_____

Picture yourself two-to-five years from now. What would you like your life to be like? What is something you want to be true? If your life were 'A dream come true' two-to-five years from now, what would it look like? Project forward several years and imagine your life is perfect in every way. What does it look like? What do you look like? What do you weigh? What kind of people are you dating? Where are you living? What are you spending your time on? Describe it as precisely as possible.

What would it take for you to be 1% happier and more fulfilled?

Imagine an area of your life you would like to improve on, an area that is challenging you. Hold that image in your mind. Write for several minutes on the question of, 'What would it look like if it were easy'?

_____

_____

_____

_____

_____

_____

_____

_____

_____

CREATING THE LIFE YOU WANT

If you don't put in any special requests to the chef, don't complain when you are served three-day-old meatloaf.

> *"There's no passion to be found in playing small, and settling for a life that is less than the one you are capable of living."*

— Nelson Mandela

> *"Your dreams are a preview of what's possible in life."*

— Ed Mylett

Exercise: CLOSE YOUR EYES FOR SEVERAL MINUTES AND THINK ABOUT WHAT IS POSSIBLE RATHER THAN WHAT IS REQUIRED

People who write down their dreams are more likely to achieve them. **In this section you will write down 'dreams that are too big' with extreme clarity.** Maybe you don't know your dream, and that's okay. Dreams are always evolving and growing, adapting just like us. If you ask very successful people about their regrets, many times they will tell you that the only thing they would change is that they would've set their goals higher.

Exercise: Write for several minutes on anything you could ever want. Write down dreams that are 'TOO BIG!'. Just go wild writing down anything you could ever want. If you see something you like, add it to this list. What would be a dream come true? What would make you wake up in the morning and be absolutely enthralled that you get to be you? What kind of a life would you be jealous of? What would your life have to be like? How much income are you earning? How much money do you have coming in passively?

Once you have filled the following pages with everything you could ever want, review the list and circle the most important among them.

_____

_____

_____

_____

_____

_____

_____

_____

_____

_____

_____

_____

_____

_____

_____

_____

_____

_____

_____

_____

_____

_____

(Wish #1:) Of one of your wishes that you circled, rewrite that wish here, and make it so clear that a child could understand it.

_____

_____

_____

(Wish #1:) Find ten people who have either done the thing you wrote down, or the closest ten people. Maybe what you wrote down has never been done before, in which case find the ten people who have done the most similar thing that you could learn from.

What do these ten people have in common? Is there something they all do?

_____

_____

_____

_____

_____

_____

_____

_____

_____

_____

_____

_____

_____

_____

_____

_____

_____

_____

_____

What must be true if you are to have Wish #1 come true? How do you move towards that? What are some steps you know you could take? Write them down, even if they're small. What would need to happen? What would it take for this wish to become a reality? What could you change in order to better align yourself with that? Who is someone who had a similar wish come true? How did they do it?

_____

_____

_____

_____

_____

_____

_____

_____

_____

_____

_____

_____

_____

_____

_____

_____

_____

_____

_____

_____

_____

_____

_____

_____

(Wish #2:) Of one of your wishes that you circled, rewrite that wish here, and make it so clear that a child could understand it.

_____

_____

_____

(Wish #2:) Find ten people who have either done the thing you wrote down, or the closest ten people. Maybe what you wrote down has never been done before, in which case find the ten people who have done the most similar thing that you could learn from.

What do these ten people have in common? Is there something they all do?

_____

_____

_____

_____

_____

_____

_____

_____

_____

_____

_____

_____

What must be true if you are to have Wish #2 come true? How do you move towards that? What are some steps you know you could take? Write them down, even if they're small. What would it take for this wish to become a reality? What could you change in order to better align yourself with that? Who is someone who had a similar wish come true? How did they do it?

_____

_____

(Wish #3:) Of one of your wishes that you circled, rewrite that wish here, and make it so clear that a child could understand it.

_____

_____

_____

(Wish #3:) Find ten people who have either done the thing you wrote down, or the closest ten people. Maybe what you wrote down has never been done before, in which case find the ten people who have done the most similar thing that you could learn from.

What do these ten people have in common? Is there something they all do?

_____

_____

_____

_____

_____

_____

_____

_____

_____

_____

_____

_____

_____

_____

What must be true if you are to have Wish #3 come true? How do you move towards that? What are some steps you know you could take? Write them down, even if they're small. What would it take for this wish to become a reality? What could you change in order to better align yourself with that? Who is someone who had a similar wish come true? How did they do it?

Exercise:

Exercise Part 1: Who do you admire most? In the boxes below, write the names of twenty people that you find inspiring, that you admire or think highly of that have some qualities or attributes you want. Then somewhere in the middle, write your name. This will help you gain clarity about who you want to be and what you want to achieve. It will also begin to shift your identity to being in alignment with what you want to achieve.

Once you are finished, write for several minutes on the key attributes/qualities you admire in these people. Identify the qualities these people have that you would like to possess or imitate. Which qualities do they possess that you can add to your own character? What are the commonalities of all of these people? Why do you want to be like them? What is it specifically that you want to add to your own character? What behaviors/attributes do you want to demonstrate? What do these people embody that you can align yourself with? When people think of you, what characteristics do you want them to think of?

(Once you have this list, look at it and ask yourself, is there anything on this list that I couldn't do?)

Exercise Part 2: In the previous exercise, you outlined people that you find most respect for. In this exercise, you will outline the opposite. Spend some time writing about the qualities that you don't want. People who have qualities and traits that disgust you. Think about the people who represent the worst qualities of humanity and those who end up with a life that nobody would want. Where do you not want to be? What are the commonalities of these people? Why do you not want to be like them? What is it specifically that you want to keep away from?

Describe these people and their qualities/decisions/life patterns below. This will help you gain clarity about who you don't want to be and what you can keep away from. _____

_____
_____
_____
_____
_____
_____
_____
_____
_____
_____
_____
_____
_____
_____
_____
_____
_____
_____
_____

Exercise: What is the most valuable thing that I can do for my community and the world over this next year? Over the next two-to-five years?

_____

_____

_____

_____

_____

_____

_____

_____

Exercise: If you could choose only one thing that you could do better, what would it be?

_____

_____

_____

_____

_____

_____

_____

_____

_____

What could you do to improve yourself?

_____

_____

_____

_____

_____

_____

_____

_____

What could you do to improve your life?

_____

_____

_____

_____

_____

_____

_____

_____

What could you do to improve the place you live, your community?

_____

_____

_____

_____

_____

_____

_____

What could you do to improve your earning capacity? Your productivity and level of value creation?

_____

_____

_____

_____

_____

_____

_____

_____

_____

What qualities, traits, behaviors, attitudes, beliefs, decisions, if you began to demonstrate, would make your life 1% better?

_____

_____

_____

_____

_____

_____

_____

_____

"A man who gives his children the habits of industry provides for them better than by giving them fortune."

— Richard Watley

Exercise: This exercise is about improving habits. What are your positive and negative habits? What could you replace them with that would be more empowering habits for you? What habits would you like to improve? If your life were everything it could be, what would your habits look like? Decide what behaviors, habits and unconscious behaviors you need to eliminate.

_____

_____

_____

_____

_____

_____

_____

_____

_____

_____

_____

_____

"Your network is your net worth."

— Anonymous

"I would rather have 1 million friends than $1 million. No, make that $100 million."

— Gary Vaynerchuk

Exercise: Spend several minutes writing before continuing on. Imagine your ideal social life and friends group in the future. What does your ideal network look like? Think about the friends you might want to have, and the type of people you might want to surround yourself with. Describe your ideal social life.

_____

_____

_____

_____

_____

_____

_____

_____

_____

_____

_____

_____

_____

_____

_____

_____

_____

_____

Exercise: Imagine your ideal personal life. What does your leisure time look like if it is set up to be fun and enjoyable for you? What do you not want to spend your free time doing?

_____

_____

_____

_____

_____

_____

_____

_____

_____

_____

_____

Exercise: Imagine and describe what your ideal family would be like. Describe it in as much detail as possible and write it in the present tense. Write about your ideal relationship with parents and siblings, spouse, children. What kind of partner would be good for you? How could you improve your relationship with your parents, siblings, spouse friends or other family?

_____

_____

_____

_____

_____

_____

_____

_____

_____

_____

_____

Keep bringing value to the marketplace and an opportunity is going to come up.

Exercise: Imagine your ideal career. How would you like to give to others? How would you like to provide value to the world? How do you want to help the people you care about? How do you want to give to the community? Where do you want to be in six months? Two years? Five years? Why? What are you trying to accomplish?

_____

_____

_____

_____

_____

_____

_____

_____

_____

_____

_____

_____

_____

What if getting up in the morning were more fun? What would make you jump out of bed in the morning?

_____

_____

_____

_____

_____

_____

_____

What would make you more 1% fulfilled? What makes you smile? What fills you with energy and lights you up? What excites you?

_____
_____
_____
_____
_____
_____

What is something you're doing wrong financially that you know you're doing wrong and that you could change that would improve your life?

_____
_____
_____
_____
_____

What is something you're doing wrong for your health, that you know you're doing wrong, that you could change that would improve your life?

_____
_____
_____
_____
_____

What is something you're doing wrong with your habits, that you know you're doing wrong, that you could change that would improve your life?

_____
_____
_____
_____
_____

What is something you're doing wrong in any area of your life, that you know you're doing wrong, that you could change that would improve your life?

_____

_____

_____

_____

_____

_____

_____

_____

What could you do today that would help take your life to another level?

- -

- -

- -

- -

- -

- -

- -

- -

If you can, visualize living your best life, and living out the highest expression of yourself as being likened to a path, and you have fallen off of that path. Ask yourself, 'What could I do to get myself back on the path I want to be on?'

_____

_____

_____

_____

_____

_____

_____

What are some small things you can do today, to begin making your life better?

_____

_____

_____

_____

_____

_____

Where have you faltered in your life? What do you need to do to begin picking up those pieces in order to turn it into a beautiful work of art?

_____

_____

_____

_____

_____

_____

_____

"*Life is suffering.*"

— Buddha

"*In some ways, suffering ceases to be suffering at the moment it finds a meaning.*"

— Victor Frankl

In this section, we will look at the most painful/darkest elements of life, and do our best to turn this darkness into light.

Exercise: Take inventory of the terrible things that have happened to you, or others, throughout human history. Ask yourself, 'What can I learn from this? How can I possibly take this terrible thing and use it to become a positive force for good? How can I turn this darkness into a little bit of light for someone else? How can I use this pain to help someone else? How can I use this pain to live a more purposeful life? How can I use this tragedy to become someone I never would have been able to before? How can I use this suffering to bring more light to the world than I ever would have been able to before?

"No matter what you're going through, this is likely not the hardest thing you've ever gone through, so you can deal with this too. If this is the hardest thing you've ever gone through, consider this: someone else has gone through something harder, and they dealt with it better than you're dealing with this right now."

— Dan Crenshaw

It has been said that meaning is the antidote to suffering. What is one thing that if it happened in the next year would make this the greatest year of your life? What would you endure any amount of suffering worth it? What is the most meaningful thing you can conceive of?

_____

_____

_____

_____

_____

_____

_____

_____

_____

_____

The million dollar question.

"The only hope I have when you look at me is you try to figure out your version of you that makes you as happy as my version of me makes me."

— Gary Vaynerchuk

If I were in charge of the educational system in America, I would make it a mandatory requirement that in order to graduate high school you must write a ten-page paper on the following question:

"If you were the best version of yourself, what would that look like?" However, if we wait to take action on what we know to be right, we perish. I don't want to perish, I want to thrive, I want you to thrive, and because of that I am presenting this exercise to you now!

In the exercise below, you will be asked to write intensely on the following question: **If you were the best version of yourself, what would that look like? What are the upper limits of who you could be?**

I believe the best gift we can give ourselves, and the people we care about, is who we become. If you have anyone or anything in this world you care about, who will you become, for them?

Exercise: This is an intense exercise. It is you versus you. It's you leveling up. This could be your hero moment. Will you take the challenge?

Who do you want to be? I have left ten pages blank for you to write on the previous bolded question. Remember, you are writing only for yourself. You are the person you decide to be. Who do you want to be?

Dream while you write; don't worry about grammar—just let your true self shine through the pages. Imagine the life that would be a dream come true, one that you would consider to be noble, honorable, exciting, heroic, legendary, etc.

If you were the best version of yourself, what would that look like? What are the upper limits of who you could be?

_____

_____

_____

_____

_____

_____

_____

_____

_____

_____
_____
_____
_____
_____
_____
_____
_____
_____
_____
_____
_____
_____
_____
_____
_____
_____
_____
_____
_____
_____
_____
_____
_____
_____
_____
_____
_____
_____
_____

Exercise part 2: At any moment you can decide what kind of a person you want to be. Do not continue on until you have made the decision to become the person you have outlined, the absolute best version of yourself. For several minutes, close your eyes and imagine you are now this version of yourself. "Mentally and visually rehearse being the person you want to be when you open your eyes." — Dr. Joe Dispenza

Exercise: Create 'I am' statements that are in alignment with this version of yourself. Write down ten 'I am' statements that are true for this version of yourself. For example, if this version of yourself represents reliability, your statement might look like, "I am reliable."

Once you have them written, say them at least once daily and feel their reality when you speak them.

Example: I am happy

1._____
_____2._____
_____3._____
_____4._____
_____5._____
_____6._____
_____7._____
_____8._____
_____9._____
_____10.____

Now that you have written your affirmations, give a one-sentence description on actions you can take related to that affirmation that begin to prove to yourself that it is true.

Example: Setting up things in your life that make you smile.

1._____
_____2._____
_____3._____
_____4._____
_____5._____
_____6._____
_____7._____
_____8._____
_____9._____
_____10.____

Exercise: What can you do today to begin acting in alignment with the version of yourself you just described?

_____
_____
_____
_____
_____
_____
_____
_____
_____

Exercise: Write down ten ideas on how you can start to live more like this version of yourself you have created.

_____
_____
_____
_____
_____
_____
_____

_____
_____
_____
_____

"If you want to see a miracle, be the miracle for someone else."

— Morgan Freeman

The pursuit itself and the progress associated is the reward.

MEDITATION JOURNAL

This page could change your life forever, and it's not what you think.

Most people have heard of meditation, but it's difficult to convince people to sit and repeat their mantra for twenty minutes. A meditation journal isn't about meditation at all. In this journal, you take any area of your life you want to reach full expression in. It could be your business, it could be a goal, it could be your finances, career, having fun, training your dog, your marriage, being great parents, coaching, etc. You take this clearly defined area of your life, let's assume for now it's fitness. You would then label the front of a journal 'Fitness'. The only thoughts allowed in this journal are those related to improving your fitness. What is your ideal body fat % range? Who is somebody that has the same level of fitness that you are seeking? How do your habits differ from theirs? What is the biggest victory you could have in your fitness right now? Who could you ask about nutrition, and a fitness plan to get where you want to go? After several minutes of writing about your fitness, it becomes very clear what you want, what you don't want, and how you can move forward to be 1% better in that area of your life.

A major reason people never get what they want is being too vague. This journal works because it helps you create extreme clarity within extremely defined areas of your life.

Exercise: Create your own meditation journal. Choose an area of your life you want to reach your full potential in, an area of your life that's important to you. Write about anything that comes to mind, write about your goals in that area, write about what you want, don't want, how you can be better, etc. Write in it at least five minutes daily. If your thoughts start to wander, course correct it back to the topic of that area. You may find that you need to create multiple meditation journals for different areas of your life.

GRATITUDE

"*Be grateful for everything that you have, and you will be successful in everything that you do.*"

— Conor Mcgregor

"*The deepest craving of human nature is the need to be appreciated.*"

— William James

"*As we express our gratitude, we must never forget that the highest appreciation is not to utter words, but to live by them.*"

— John F. Kennedy

"*Be thankful for what you have; you'll end up having more. If you concentrate on what you don't have, you will never, ever have enough.*"

— Oprah Winfrey

"*I awoke this morning with devout gratitude for my friends, the old and the new. Cultivate the habit of being grateful for every good thing that comes to you, and to give thanks continuously. And because all things have contributed to your advancement, you should include all things in your gratitude.*"

— Ralph Waldo Emerson

"Strive to find things to be thankful for, and just look for the good in who you are."

— Bethany Hamilton

"When you are grateful, fear disappears and abundance appears."

— Anthony Robbins

"Gratitude and attitude are not challenges, they are choices."

— Robert Braathe

"Reflect upon your present blessings, of which every man has many."

— Charles Dickens

"The secret to wealth is gratitude. If you have a billion dollars, but every day you live pissed off and frustrated, the quality of your life is pissed off and frustrated. If you have nothing, but you're euphorically grateful for whatever you have, you're the richest person in the world."

— John Templeton

Exercise: Identify what is most important in your life. Write down what is most important to you, and feel the gratitude power in that as you write.

_____

_____

_____

_____

_____

_____

_____

Exercise: Each day for the next ten days, do something each day to show someone that you appreciate them; share your gratitude with them. You may think this is beneficial just to them, but it's actually beneficial to both of you. If you show your gratitude for someone for doing a certain thing, that acts as a reward, and they are more likely to do it again!

Exercise: Close your eyes for three minutes and focus on three things you are most grateful for in your life.

EPIC BUCKET LIST

Exercise: Create your own EPIC bucket list! Everyone has a limited amount of time on earth. What do you want to do before you die? If anything were possible, what would you do? Who would you be? What do you want to do with your time on this earth? Write down anything you've ever really wanted to do, be or have. Example ideas you may choose: Meet Harry Potter, graduate high school, give a TED talk, start a family, be the most reliable person you know, travel to fifty countries, run a marathon, own a car wash, throw out the first pitch at the world series, visit the Grand Canyon, etc.

_____

_____

_____

_____

_____

_____

_____

_____

_____

_____

_____

_____

_____

_____

_____

_____

_____

Model The Best

"Find somebody who is where you want to be. Study what they do. Every aspect of what they do. Add yourself to it."

— Tony Robbins

"Reg Park was someone I looked up to and I followed his training principles."

— Arnold Schwarzenegger

"Success leaves clues."

— Anonymous

If you think what the best think, do what the best do, eat what the best eat, and feel what the best feel, and combine that with your own uniqueness over a long enough time period, you are the best.

Getting what we want isn't complex. Much of what we want, other people have already been there, and because of that we can study what they did, and learn from them. To get what you want, align yourself with the most proven plan available, or imagine what the most proven plan would look like, and follow that.

As our society progresses, models become more clear. If you go to the doctor with a broken leg, they know how to treat it because broken legs have been treated for thousands of years. It is easier to get

112

into good shape in 2022 than it was in 1922 because more is known about health and nutrition today than it was a hundred years ago. **Don't reinvent the wheel. Find people who have already gone where you want to be. Find somebody who is where you want to be, and do what they did with slight improvement. Find the proven plan and make it slightly better.** That is how progress happens. If what you are doing has never been done before, find the people who have gone the farthest and seek counsel from them. As you move into uncharted territory and there is no model to guide you, you must imagine what the model would look like if you were having the success you wanted, and follow that.

Other examples of models:

Self Development: Tony Robbins is arguably the greatest self-development coach on the planet. His mentor was the legendary Jim Rohn, the self-development legend of his era.

Football: Kirk Ferentz has been the head coach @Iowa for 20+ years. He has three sons, and all three of them played football for him, and went on to have various coaching positions in the NFL.

Peyton Manning and Eli Manning are among the greatest quarterbacks of the modern era. Their father, Archie Manning, was a professional quarterback as well. Arch Manning is the grandson of Archie Manning and is ranked as one of the top players in the nation.

(https://www.si.com/college/olemiss/football/archie-talks-arch-manning-ole-miss-college-recruitment)

Aidan Hutchinson: As a senior in 2021 for Michigan, Hutchinson set the team's single-season sack record at fourteen. Almost thirty years prior, his father Chris Hutchinson tied the then-school record with eleven.

(https://en.wikipedia.org/wiki/Michigan_Wolverines_football_statistical_leaders#Sacks)

Rams head coach Sean McVay became the youngest head coach to win the Lombardi Trophy. His grandfather, **John McVay,** won five

Super Bowl rings as a front office executive in personnel with the San Francisco 49ers.

(https://www.foxsports.com/stories/nfl/super-bowl-2022-sean-mcvay-cooper-kupp-talk-family-rams-repeat)

Basketball: There are countless father-son duos in basketball. Greg/Doug McDermott: Greg is the head basketball coach at Creighton, and has held numerous other coaching positions at successful institutions. Doug has a career NBA three-point % above 40%.

Stephen Curry and his brother Seth Curry are both among the NBA's all time great three point shooters; their father had a decade-long NBA career.

(https://thelistwire.usatoday.com/lists/syracuse-university-jim-boeheim-buddy-boeheim-fathers-who-coached-their-sons-in-college-basketball/)

Business: Henry Ford II, the grandson of Henry Ford, went on to become the CEO of Ford Motor Company. There are many examples of high level executive positions being passed down through families.

Politics: Bill Clinton was the 42nd President of the United States of America. Hillary Clinton ran, and lost to Donald Trump in the running for the 45th Presidency. Was Hillary Clinton a better candidate than many other Americans? Maybe not, but she had the model. She had the blueprint of 'How to win the U.S. Presidency'. The lesson we can take from her loss is: models are always adapting and getting more efficient, and if you aren't constantly adapting your model of success, you're falling behind.

To those who are cynical and think, 'Oh, must be nice, Daddy/Mommy got them the job', or 'must be nice having connections', you are missing the point. It's not that these people were handed the job or the life, or the success on a silver platter. They were handed the recipe, and once you have the recipe, virtually anyone who meets the minimum requirements can bake it. The perfectly defined model is the ability to say, 'do this, do this, add a little bit of this, and this is the result you will get.' In this next exercise you will be asked to define your own model.

Exercise: What is the current model of success in your desired field? What does a 1% better model look like? If you were to have a revolutionary breakthrough, what would it look like? What is your cake you're trying to create? What do you want it to look like when you're done? What result are you after? What would the recipe of that cake look like?

_____

_____

_____

_____

_____

_____

_____

_____

_____

_____

_____

_____

_____

_____

_____

_____

_____

_____

Find somebody who has taken your model the farthest, and obsessively learn from them. This relationship is often more valuable than the success you achieve after all.

Thoughts on various models: Successful people become extremely skilled in their ability to find, and act in alignment with working models. Now that you have defined your model, how do you begin working in alignment with it?

_____

_____

_____

_____

_____

_____

_____

_____

_____

_____

_____

_____

_____

_____

_____

_____

_____

_____

_____

_____

_____

_____

WHICH PILL WILL YOU TAKE?

If you gave me the choice, and put in front of me a red pill and a blue pill, and when you take the blue pill $10 billion cash is immediately transferred to your bank account, and when you take the red pill you become the absolute best version of yourself that is possible, I would take the red pill every time. If I had the choice of giving you one billion dollars, or giving you an obsession with becoming the best version of yourself, I would choose to give you the latter.

Exercise: What is your red pill/blue pill? What do you truly want to create? What kind of life do you want to live? What kind of life do you not want to live?